Explode The Code 3½

Nancy Hall
Rena Price

If I sneeze, will I scare the bee?

Educators Publishing Service, Inc.
Cambridge, Mass. 02138-1104

Cover by Hugh Price.
Text Illustrations by Andrew Mockler.

CONTENTS

Lesson 1

If a word has **e** at the end, the **e** is silent and the vowel before it says its name.

rod/rode

○ it:

bon
(bone)
ban

drive
Dave
dive

bask
bank
bake

sole
Sal
sale

tire
tine
tin

pave
pink
poke

game
get
gate

mile
mill
melt

1

○ it:

rod or (rode?)	mine or nine?
dine or dime?	vine or van?
ton or tune?	wade or wad?
can or cane?	bite or bike?
Kate or cat?	file or fill?

2

Read, write, and "X" it:

1.	rode <u>rode</u>			
2.	wade _____			
3.	tune _____			
4.	dive _____			
5.	cave _____			
6.	bone _____			
7.	tire _____			

3

Match and write it:

nine   bake   bike   gate   poke

sale   fire   vine   ~~mule~~   bite

mule

_____

_____

_____

_____

_____

_____

	Spell:				Write:
1.		n ⓡ ⓞ e	be ⓓⓔ		*rode*
2.		b d o i	te de		
3.		p b a o	ke k		
4.		r c i a	v ve		
5.		w m u a	d de		
6.		p d e i	me ne		
7.		n r o a	d de		

Yes or No?

		Yes	No
1.	Can you swim in a dry cave?	☐	☒
2.	Will a dog ask for a bone at the store?	☐	☐
3.	Can you ride a bike fast?	☐	☐
4.	Is it fun to wade in a lake?	☐	☐
5.	Will you bite Kate if she pokes you?	☐	☐
6.	Can a mule bake a cake?	☐	☐
7.	Will you wipe your hands on your robe?	☐	☐

"X" it:

1.	Bob had nine dimes and gave me five. ☒ Babs will dine at nine by the fire. ☐	
2.	Jane rides the mule past the gate. ☐ The mule rides Jane past the gate. ☐	
3.	Matt rode home with his pet. ☐ Matt's pet rode home on the bike. ☐	
4.	Lin pokes in the damp cave. ☐ Lin puts out the fire in the dry cave. ☐	
5.	Kate likes to wade in the mud hole. ☐ Kate waves to Mom from home base. ☐	
6.	Dave will take lots of time to fix the tire. ☐ Dave will take the last rose on the vine. ☐	
7.	Win has a bone the size of a log. ☐ Our side wins the home game. ☐	HOME VISITOR 9 2

Write it, using a word with silent **e** at the end:

1.		*wade* _____
2.		_____
3.		_____
4.		_____
5.		_____
6.		_____
7.		_____

Lesson 2

If a word has a silent **e** at the end, the vowel says its name.

⃝ it:

grade globe glide	stone stole stale
blame blade blob	drink bride drive
brave broke brake	dress blaze glaze
desk base doze	pass past paste

glib   or   glide?

class   or   close?

skate   or   scare?

scare   or   scale?

globe   or   glad?

spare   or   spade?

fame   or   frame?

trade   or   trap?

stone   or   stove?

prize   or   print?

Read, write, and "X" it:

1. drive _____			
2. smoke _____			
3. prize _____			
4. globe _____			
5. paste _____			
6. brave _____			
7. scale _____			

Match and write it:

smoke	scare	close	drive	trade
stone	blade	frame	bride	spade

smoke   scare   close   drive   trade
stone   blade   frame   bride   spade

_____

_____

_____

_____

_____

_____

_____

_____

1.		pl sm	e	o	ke pe	_____
2.		cl gl	o	a	se be	_____
3.		br dr	i	a	ve de	_____
4.		st sc	a	o	re le	_____
5.		sl st	o	u	le ve	_____
6.		pr pl	e	i	ze ne	_____
7.		fl fr	u	a	ne me	_____

Yes or No?

	Yes	No
1. Is it fun to slide on a wide slope?	☐	☐
2. Can you stop a blaze if you doze?	☐	☐
3. Can she get a prize if she skates well?	☐	☐
4. Will a bride toss her ring in the wind?	☐	☐
5. Can a pup scare a pile of logs?	☐	☐
6. Is it brave to get help if you smell smoke?	☐	☐
7. If you are nine, will you be in tenth grade?	☐	☐

14

"X" it:

#			
1.	The bride slides into the plate on a base hit.	☐	
	The bride hates to wipe the pile of plates.	☐	
2.	Fran dines with a snake in the grass.	☐	
	Fran drives home to get a late snack.	☐	
3.	Steve will vote for his pal to win the prize.	☐	
	The prize bull has Steve in the ring.	☐	
4.	White smoke came from the blaze on the stove.	☐	
	The name of the big, white dog is Blaze.	☐	
5.	Dave smiles as he steps on the scale.	☐	
	Dave has miles to go to get home.	☐	
6.	Mame closes the lid with a bang.	☐	
	Mame bangs pot lids in the jazz band.	☐	
7.	The brave pup scares the men as they doze.	☐	
	The brave men scare the bats with a hose.	☐	

Write it, using a word with silent **e** at the end:

1. _____

2. _____

3. _____

4. _____

5. _____

6. _____

7. _____

Lesson 3

-**ck** at the end of a word says / k / as in bla**ck**.
-**ng** at the end of a word says / ng / as in ki**ng**.

◯ it:

drink ring bring	dock duke duck
blush back block	wing ring rung
lung luck lick	shack trash track
sting stick sick	game long gong

○ it:

flag or fling?	log or long?
back or black?	pick or pack?
rang or rank?	lock or clock?
swung or stung?	stink or stick?
slick or sling?	sing or wing?

Read, write, and "X" it:

1. dock
   _____

2. bring
   _____

3. long
   _____

4. block
   _____

5. gong
   _____

6. clock
   _____

7. sing
   _____

19

Match and write it:

black   pick   lick   bring   bike
duck   dock   stack   swung   king

_____

_____

_____

_____

_____

_____

_____

_____

	Spell:				Write:
1.		br tr	i a	ck st	_____
2.		bl pl	a o	nk ck	_____
3.		br dr	o i	ng nk	_____
4.		b d	u o	sk ck	_____
5.		sw sl	e i	ng nk	_____
6.		s r	e a	ng r	_____
7.		st sl	a i	nk ck	_____

Yes or No?

	Yes	No
1. Will you have a snack with a skunk?	☐	☐
2. Can you make a kite go up in the sky?	☐	☐
3. Will a duck use its wings to fly?	☐	☐
4. Does a block tell you the time?	☐	☐
5. Will a rock sink in a lake?	☐	☐
6. Can you sing and swing with a pal?	☐	☐
7. Will a duck help pick up the junk?	☐	☐

"X" it:

1.	Bing can sing a tune like a king. ☐ The king likes to sit on the swing. ☐	
2.	The duck has a ring in its bill. ☐ The duck makes a ring with the hose. ☐	
3.	Frank can lift the long, black bike. ☐ Frank left his back tire at the dump. ☐	
4.	A string and some sticks can make a kite. ☐ Stan flings the stick off the dock in the lake. ☐	
5.	The gang brings skates to the rink. ☐ The gong rings for Bing to go to class. ☐	
6.	The black duck honks in the strong wind. ☐ The truck honks at the duck on the bike. ☐	
7.	Jane swung the bat with a bang and made a hit. ☐ The bat dives at Jane and flaps its wings. ☐	

Write it, using a word with **ck** or **ng**:

1.

2.

3.

4.

5.

6.

7.

Lesson 4

sh says / sh / as in **sh**ell.

$\bigcirc$ it:

	trash crash rash		self shell shelf
	shape shade shop		slash splash shall
	hats hash hush		ranch rush rash
	cash cats shack		shams smash small

○ it:

rush or rash?	gas or gash?
blush or brush?	shin or shine?
shack or sack?	track or trash?
shelf or shell?	lush or slush?
sake or shake?	sift or shift?

Read, write, and "X" it:

1.	shade _____			
2.	ship _____			
3.	fish _____			
4.	shelf _____			
5.	trash _____			
6.	crash _____			
7.	hush _____			

Match and write it:

dash   crash   brush   mash   slush
cash   splash   shine   fresh   shack

_____

_____

_____

_____

_____

_____

_____

_____

28

	Spell:			Write:
1.	r n	a o	ss sh	_____
2.	st sh	i e	ll lf	_____
3.	sh shr	o i	mp p	_____
4.	s sh	u a	sh ke	_____
5.	s sh	o a	pe de	_____
6.	sn sm	a e	sh ps	_____
7.	d b	i a	s sh	_____

Yes or No?

	Yes No
1. Can you get cash at a bank?	☐ ☐
2. Is an ant the size of a shelf?	☐ ☐
3. Can I grab a fresh plum at the store?	☐ ☐
4. Does a ship get a rash from the sun?	☐ ☐
5. Will I get a gash on the shin if the puck hits me?	☐ ☐
6. If I splash in the fresh mud, will I be dry?	☐ ☐
7. If I sit in the shade, will I get a tan?	☐ ☐

"X" it:

1.	The ship will smash into the dock and snap its mast. ☐ Doc slaps Skip on the back and smiles. ☐	
2.	Sol will dive into the lake and splash his pal. ☐ Pete will splash gas as he fills up his truck. ☐	
3.	We can find him if his red nose will flash and shine. ☐ The red flash tells the truck to stop. ☐	
4.	The shade of the lamp fell off and broke. ☐ Luke broke his leg as he fell off the ship. ☐	
5.	The spy will flash an S.O.S. for help. ☐ The flash in the sky scares us. ☐	
6.	The doll on the shelf can sing a tune. ☐ The crab will dash to the shell to be safe. ☐	
7.	He will crush nuts and shake them on the cake. ☐ Why did Ric sit on the cake and crush it? ☐	

Write it, using a word with **sh**:

1.		_____
2.		_____
3.		_____
4.		_____
5.		_____
6.		_____
7.		_____

Lesson 5

ch says / ch / as in **ch**op.
tch at the end of a word says / ch / as in ma**tch**.

◯ it:

	chunk chums chin		sash shack snatch
	cast chest chill		much mush munch
	chess scotch sketch		bench branch bank
	stick stink stitch		champ camp shine

◯ it:

champ or hump?	pitch or pinch?
stitch or still?	mast or match?
wish or witch?	check or chick?
chap or chop?	close or chose?
chums or hum?	hash or hatch?

Read, write, and "X" it:

1.	ranch _____			
2.	champ _____			
3.	sketch _____			
4.	pinch _____			
5.	crutch _____			
6.	chest _____			
7.	chess _____			

Match and write it:

witch	ranch	chums	hatch	champ
stitch	pitch	munch	branch	sketch

_____

_____

_____

_____

_____

_____

_____

_____

	Spell:			Write:
1.	n m	an un	ch sh	_____
2.	p b	in em	st ch	_____
3.	ch sh	o a	nk mp	_____
4.	ch sh	i e	ss ck	_____
5.	n m	o a	tch sh	_____
6.	ch sh	a o	p g	_____
7.	sn sh	a e	ck tch	_____

37

Yes or No?

	Yes	No
1. Will a chick hatch from its shell?	☐	☐
2. Can a stitch be made in a dish?	☐	☐
3. Will a champ try to win the prize?	☐	☐
4. Can I grab a fresh plum from a branch?	☐	☐
5. Will you get rich if you sell trash?	☐	☐
6. Does a branch get a rash from the sun?	☐	☐
7. Can you sketch a mad witch?	☐	☐

"X" it:

1.	Jen sticks tacks in the long bench.	☐	
	A long branch is stuck on the tracks.	☐	
2.	The king uses a blade to chop his logs.	☐	
	The shy king longs to have a chum.	☐	
3.	The crutch sticks on the end of the stiff branch.	☐	
	The chums stick the branch in the trash.	☐	
4.	Did Chet pinch his skin in the latch of the chest?	☐	
	The latch on the chest is stuck shut.	☐	
5.	My rich chum shines his lamp in the back of the cave.	☐	
	My rich chum has a chunk of cash in the bank.	☐	
6.	The bride hangs her ring on a branch.	☐	
	The bride ropes a black bull in the ring.	☐	
7.	Chong ducks as Skip flings his lunch at him.	☐	
	Chong makes a sketch of the ducks in the pond.	☐	

Write it, using a word with **ch** or **tch**:

1. _____

2. _____

3. _____

4. _____

5. _____

6. _____

7. _____

Lesson 6

wh says / wh / as in **wh**ip.

◯ it:

	while whale wall		whet whit white
	what wing wink		wed when web
	wake wash whack		wine whine whim
	wag whig witch		whiff wish wisk

41

◯ it:

when or win?	wig or wipe?
wine or whine?	chose or whose?
white or while?	wish or which?
ham or wham?	wink or woke?
whip or whim?	whack or shack?

Read, write, and "X" it:

1.	whiff _____			
2.	wink _____			
3.	whine _____			
4.	whack _____			SUNDAY - - - - MONDAY - - - - TUESDAY - - - - WEDNESDAY - - - THURSDAY - - - FRIDAY - - - - - SATURDAY - - -
5.	whale _____			
6.	whip _____			
7.	wham _____			

Match and write it:

whiff   chose   whip   white   witch

wink   whack   whale   wipe   whine

Spell: Write:

#		Spell			Write
1.		wh ch	a u	m t	_____
2.		sh wh	o i	p b	_____
3.		ch wh	i o	ss ff	_____
4.		wh sh	i a	le ll	_____
5.		w wh	e u	b d	_____
6.		wh sh	a e	ke ck	_____
7.		m w	i a	ck ke	_____

Yes or No?

		Yes	No
1.	Will a pup whine to get a snack?	☐	☐
2.	Will a whale wipe its wet hands?	☐	☐
3.	If you whack your best pal, will the pal grin?	☐	☐
4.	Can you get a whiff when you bake a cake?	☐	☐
5.	Do you wish you had a white wig?	☐	☐
6.	When you play chess, do you like to win?	☐	☐
7.	If I pitch the ball, will you wham it?	☐	☐

"X" it:

1.	At lunch a bunch of whales dive for fish.	☐	
	The whale will fry a hot dog for lunch.	☐	
2.	The champ whips the egg whites for his prize cake.	☐	
	When the white eggs hatch, the chicks will be wet.	☐	
3.	Nan whines and then sobs when she must drink her milk.	☐	
	Win whines to go chase the cat in the grass.	☐	
4.	Which twin will use a hose on the fire?	☐	
	Which twin has a rash on his nose?	☐	
5.	Why does it take so long to split a log?	☐	
	Why do you splash Sis when it is hot?	☐	
6.	Jon whips the eggs to make the cake.	☐	
	The cake which Jon made has five sides.	☐	
7.	The white rat winks at the cute cat.	☐	
	When the rat yells, the white pig saves it.	☐	

Write it, using a word with **wh**:

1.

   _____

2.

   _____

3.

   _____

4.

   _____

5.

   _____

6.

   _____

7.

   _____

Lesson 7

th says / th / as in **th**ink.

◯ it:

	thump think lump		hatch snatch thatch
	chick tick thick		bath dash date
	tank thank think		thumb thug than
	match mash math		throne tone then

49

○ it:

tank or thank?	Beth or bath?
bath or path?	thing or think?
this or wish?	pat or path
match or math?	then or ten?
thick or think?	chin or thin?

Read, write, and "X" it:

1. thump _____			
2. thing _____			
3. thin _____			
4. thick _____			
5. thug _____			
6. math _____			
7. think _____			

Match and write it:

path   tug   than   bath   thick

throne   Beth   tan   think   thank

1.		b d	o a	th ch	_____
2.		th wh	a u	mp le	_____
3.		ch th	e i	nk ck	_____
4.		wh th	u i	ne ng	_____
5.		n m	a o	tch th	_____
6.		sh th	e i	n nt	_____
7.		wh th	n u	th g	_____

Yes or No?

	Yes	No
1. Will you thank a thug who mugs you?	☐	☐
2. Will you wish for the best grade in math?	☐	☐
3. Do you think a bath is fun to take?	☐	☐
4. Is your pal as thin as you?	☐	☐
5. Will a duck land on top of a king's throne?	☐	☐
6. Do you think your name is swell?	☐	☐
7. Does your dog go with you to class?	☐	☐

"X" it:

1.	Ted flings a dish of figs at the thug. ☐ The thug brings Ted some fish on a dish. ☐		
2.	Beth wins the prize in math class. ☐ Beth flings her cash in the trash can. ☐		
3.	The odd thing in the shack scares me. ☐ This odd thing has a thin, white shell. ☐		
4.	Kim thinks the swing will crash. ☐ Kim thanks the king for the cash. ☐		
5.	The path to the shack is in the sand dunes. ☐ Jane piles things in a stack on the sand. ☐		
6.	The champ sings when he takes a bath. ☐ The chimp makes a pink ring on the rug. ☐		
7.	Chan sits on the throne and thinks he is king. ☐ The king thanks Chan for help with his math. ☐		

Write it, using a word with **th**:

1. _____

2. _____

3. _____

4. _____

5. _____

6. _____

7. _____

Lesson 8   Review Lesson

◯ it:	smock smoke slope		fling sling flag
	chimp thump slump		thine shone whine
	whack while whale		clam shin chums
	wine vine vim		drench branch brain
	cling clang clog		freak trash fresh

○ it:

sped or spade?	shell or spill?
paste or past?	shake or shape?
track or tack?	camp or champ?
crust or crush?	pitch or gift?
mule or mull?	rash or trash?

Read, write, and "X" it:

1.	track _____			
2.	chase _____			
3.	smash _____			
4.	chop _____			
5.	spill _____			
6.	sling _____			
7.	shade _____			

Match and write it:

shape   fresh   whine   chums   chase

tack   branch   thump   smash   track

	Spell:			Write:
1.	sh ch	o a	de be	_____
2.	w m	i u	le ne	_____
3.	br tr	a e	sh ck	_____
4.	sp sl	u a	de pe	_____
5.	w wh	a e	lp le	_____
6.	p h	a e	ste sk	_____
7.	sh ch	u o	d p	_____

61

Yes or No?

	Yes	No
1. Will a whale have a snack with you?	☐	☐
2. Is a chum the same as a pal?	☐	☐
3. Will paste help to fix a rip in your pants?	☐	☐
4. Can you use a spade to dig?	☐	☐
5. Will a long vine stretch up to the sky?	☐	☐
6. Can I lift the trash with a string?	☐	☐
7. Can a moth fly as fast as a plane?	☐	☐

"X" it:

1.	Chad puts the trash in the stove.	☐	
	Chad takes the trash from the shack.	☐	
2.	The big cat has a hunch that Beth will win the chess game.	☐	
	Beth has lunch with the big white cat.	☐	
3.	Jane whacks the fire with a wet branch.	☐	
	Jane winks at the thing and gives it a pinch.	☐	
4.	The snake hides on the bench in the shade.	☐	
	The pet will push the odd thing on the swing.	☐	
5.	The chums fill the chest with fresh fish.	☐	
	The chess king spoke to the chums.	☐	
6.	The duck thumps its wings when it sings well.	☐	
	The duck broke its wing and had to use a crutch.	☐	
7.	The ranch makes a grand spot for a thug to hide.	☐	
	Beth rakes the long grass at the ranch.	☐	

Write it:

1. _____

2. _____

3. _____

4. _____

5. _____

6. _____

7. _____

Lesson 9

ee says /ē/ as in b**ee**.

◯ it:

seeds seem seek	feel heel heed
cheap sheet sheer	speed peek peel
grease goes geese	freed trees freeze
sleep sleeve sleet	SUNDAY - - - - MONDAY - - - - TUESDAY - - - - WEDNESDAY - - - THURSDAY - - - FRIDAY - - - - - SATURDAY - - - week walk wick

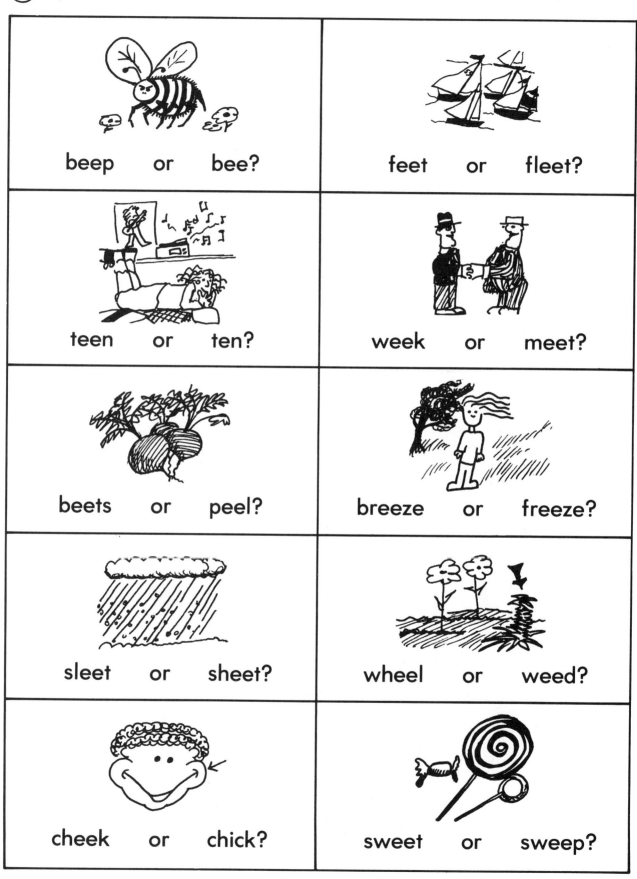

beep or bee?	feet or fleet?
teen or ten?	week or meet?
beets or peel?	breeze or freeze?
sleet or sheet?	wheel or weed?
cheek or chick?	sweet or sweep?

Read, write, and "X" it:

1.	cheek _____	✔		
2.	wheel _____			SUNDAY - - - - MONDAY - - - - TUESDAY - - - - WEDNESDAY - - - THURSDAY - - - FRIDAY - - - - - SATURDAY - - -
3.	sheep _____			
4.	keep _____			
5.	speed _____		Hi!	
6.	speech _____			
7.	street _____			

Match and write it:

speed   eel   sweet   weep   cheek
heel   freeze   geese   sleeve   keep

_____
_____
_____

_____
_____
_____

_____
_____
_____

_____
_____
_____

_____
_____
_____

_____
_____
_____

_____
_____
_____

_____
_____
_____

Spell: Write:

#		Spell			Write
1.		wh th	e ee	l p	_____
2.		ch sh	i ee	p d	_____
3.		w m	ee a	sh k	_____
4.		m n	i ee	lk t	_____
5.		d b	a ee		_____
6.		sh ch	ee e	t k	_____
7.		b h	a ee	t l	_____

Yes or No?

	Yes	No
1. Will you be a teen in a week?	☐	☐
2. Will I scare the bee if I sneeze?	☐	☐
3. Do geese sleep when they fly?	☐	☐
4. Can a cone be sweet to taste?	☐	☐
5. Will a deer wish to drive a jeep?	☐	☐
6. Will sheep need sheets on the bed?	☐	☐
7. Can you keep a clock on the shelf?	☐	☐

"X" it:

1.	The bee spent a week on the bench.	☐	
	The bee spends cash for a sweet snack.	☐	
2.	The geese will fly with top speed.	☐	
	The fleet will go fast in the breeze.	☐	
3.	Dee thinks the weed makes her sneeze.	☐	
	Dee will sleep for more than a week.	☐	
4.	The deer feels safe in the tree.	☐	
	The deer feed on cake and sweets.	☐	
5.	The teen speeds up the wide street.	☐	
	The teen sleeps on white sheets.	☐	
6.	Lee hangs the sheets on the line to dry.	☐	
	Lee has long sleeves on her best dress.	☐	
7.	Bo Peep cheers when she sees her lost sheep.	☐	
	The lost sheep weep when they can't find Bo's street.	☐	

Write it, using a word with **ee**:

#		
1.		_____
2.		_____
3.	SUNDAY - - - - MONDAY - - - - TUESDAY - - - - WEDNESDAY - - - THURSDAY - - - FRIDAY - - - - - SATURDAY - - -	_____
4.		_____
5.		_____
6.		_____
7.		_____

Lesson 10

ea says /ē/ as in **ea**t.

◯ it:

	feat feast flea		sneak seat seeds
	yeast fear year		leak freak leap
	team steam tear		clear cheap cheat
	pear beak peak		patch beam beach

73

○ it:

year or fear?	leap or leaf?
each or east?	clear or cheer?
weave or weak?	sneak or steam?
beast or beans?	tease or tea?
leave or lead?	ear or eat?

Read, write, and "X" it:

1.	grease _____			
2.	peach _____			
3.	meat _____			
4.	beast _____			
5.	weak _____			
6.	leaf _____			
7.	teach _____			

75

Match and write it:

leaf   ear   peak   sneak   near

beach   team   fear   meat   cheap

		Spell:			Write:
1.		s sh	ea e	d t	_____
2.		cl l	a ea	d p	_____
3.		h y	ea a	r p	_____
4.		ea i	ch st		_____
5.		p b	e ea	sh ch	_____
6.		sl fl	o ea		_____
7.		d b	ea oa	rs st	_____

Yes or No?

	Yes	No
1. Is a week as long as a year?	☐	☐
2. Do you cheer to help the home team win?	☐	☐
3. Do you see steam when you make tea?	☐	☐
4. Can a flea teach me to fly?	☐	☐
5. Can you give each of your pals a treat?	☐	☐
6. Is it fun to leap in a pile of leaves?	☐	☐
7. Will a path to the east lead you west?	☐	☐

"X" it:

1.	The flea puts paste on the seat. ☐ The flea puts the meat on the scale. ☐	
2.	Jean will go to the beach when it is clear. ☐ Jean weaves cheap mats to sell. ☐	
3.	The team cheers from the rear of the bus. ☐ The team has a treat to eat at the game. ☐	
4.	Dean shears the sheep on the ranch. ☐ Dean sneaks a plate from the top shelf. ☐	
5.	The gang of teens rides ten-speed bikes. ☐ Each of the twins likes to read. ☐	
6.	The class cheers at the end of the year. ☐ Each year the class hears the band. ☐	
7.	The beast leaps from the dock to the sea. ☐ A leaf from the tree drops on the beast. ☐	

Write it, using a word with **ea**:

1. _____

2. _____

3. _____

4. _____

5. _____

6. _____

7. _____

ay says /ā/ as in pl**ay**.
ay is often at the end of a word.

◯ it:

gray bray pray	day clap clay
ray Fay lay	gray tray trait
hay pay may	way slay say
day bay bray	bag play pay

81

○ it:

stay or stag?	bay or day?
Fay or fog?	pay or play?
gray or grease?	jog or jay?
stay or stray?	sway or clay?
way or wag?	lag or lay?

Read, write, and "X" it:

1. clay _____			
2. ray _____			
3. jay _____			
4. day _____			
5. lay _____			
6. play _____			
7. spray _____			

Match and write it:

Fay   stray   play   sway   clay
say   stay   day   bay   pay

_____

_____

_____

_____

_____

_____

_____

_____

	Spell:			Write:
1.		st h	ai ay		_____
2.		hr tr	ai ay		_____
3.		c cl	ay a	ve d	_____
4.		r b	ay ea		_____
5.		st spr	ai ay		_____
6.		cl c	ay a	ne s	_____
7.		pr dr	ai ay		_____

Yes or No?

	Yes	No
1. Is it fun to make shapes with clay?	☐	☐
2. Will a train fit on a tray?	☐	☐
3. Do you eat weeds and hay for lunch?	☐	☐
4. Will your dog stay when you tell him to?	☐	☐
5. Must we pay for a ray of sun?	☐	☐
6. Will you spray the truck to get it clean?	☐	☐
7. Have you seen a hen lay fresh eggs?	☐	☐

"X" it:

1. Jay cleans his bike with the spray can. ☐

   Jay gets the top prize for his clay pot. ☐

2. The chicks stay near the tent. ☐

   The chicks play tag in the hay. ☐

3. The gray mule will try to chase Gay. ☐

   Gay chose to ride the gray mule. ☐

4. She sees a way to reach the trays. ☐

   The box of eggs will slide off the desk. ☐

5. Ray wipes milk from **the** gray dog's chin. ☐

   Ray wipes gray mud and clay off his bike. ☐

6. The class plays on the steep slope. ☐

   The cast must stay on his leg till it heals. ☐

7. The stray pup plays near the street. ☐

   The duck chose a bad spot to lay an egg. ☐

Write it, using a word with **ay** at the end:

1.	_____
2.	_____
3.	_____
4.	_____
5.	_____
6.	_____
7.	_____

Lesson 12

ai says /ā/ as in tr**ai**n.
ai is at the beginning or middle of a word.

 it:

	beat brain bait		mail maid nail
	smack sail snail		tail rail trail
	paid trade braids		rain drain dream
	pain fail Spain		green grain gain

○ it:

mast or waist?	mail or maid?
fail or fall?	paint or plant?
trim or train?	fair or faint?
raid or rain?	trail or tail?
jail or gain?	pair or pain?

90

Read, write, and "X" it:

1.	aim _____			
2.	sail _____			
3.	waist _____			
4.	pail _____			
5.	gain _____			
6.	air _____			
7.	pair _____			

91

Match and write it:

pain	said	drain	jail	rain
snail	braids	air	sail	pail

92

	Spell:				Write:
1.		ch sh	ai ay	r n	_____
2.		tr t	ee ai	n l	_____
3.		m n	a ai	t l	_____
4.		m r	ea ai	n d	_____
5.		sn s	ee ai	l f	_____
6.		b p	ai a	ne nt	_____
7.		br tr	ea ai	r n	_____

Yes or No?

		Yes	No
1.	Will it rain if the sky is fair?	☐	☐
2.	Can you fix your hair in braids?	☐	☐
3.	Will a nail feel pain if it is bent?	☐	☐
4.	Will you cheer if you fail a test?	☐	☐
5.	Will gray paint be kept in a can?	☐	☐
6.	Is it a prize to go to jail?	☐	☐
7.	Can geese go as fast as a plane?	☐	☐

"X" it:

1.	The pup's tail is stuck in the fresh paint. ☐ The bad pup puts paint in the sink drain. ☐	
2.	The maid likes to fish with live bait in the tub. ☐ The fish thinks the maid's braids are fine bait. ☐	
3.	Craig's belt makes a pain in his waist. ☐ Craig's waist is too thin for Dad's pants. ☐	
4.	Gail fails to reach the train in time. ☐ Gail can see the trail as she waits for her pal. ☐	
5.	The pair of snails goes to the beach for the day. ☐ The pair of wet sails goes on the line to dry. ☐	
6.	Chet sits on the rail to wait for the mail. ☐ Chet waits in the jeep for the rain to stop. ☐	
7.	The big wheel takes the chums up in the air. ☐ Chuck's bike tire needs more air. ☐	

Write it, using a word with **ai** in the middle:

1. _____

2. _____

3. _____

4. _____

5. _____

6. _____

7. _____

ow says /ō/ as in cr**ow**.
ow is often at the end of a word.

◯ it:

	grab gross grow		slow stow show
	snow slow slaw		log low tow
	flow blow from		crow now row
	slow snow show		glove grow glow

row or crow?	blow or bow?
now or own?	snow or shot?
bowl or blow?	tow or throw?
mow or row?	slow or snow?
two or tow?	flew or flow?

Read, write, and "X" it:

1.	crow _____			
2.	blow _____			
3.	flow _____			
4.	snow _____			
5.	mow _____			
6.	glow _____			
7.	row _____			

Match and write it:

bow   grow   flow   blow   low
show   slow   throw   row   snow

	Spell:		Write:
1.	r t	ee ow	_____
2.	gr pl	ow ea	_____
3.	sw sl	ow a	_____
4.	dr cr	ay ow	_____
5.	thr tr	ow eu	_____
6.	sh sn	a ow	_____
7.	d b	o ow	_____

Yes or No?

	Yes	No
1. Will a duck wish to row with a stick?	☐	☐
2. Do we mow the grass when it snows?	☐	☐
3. Will a truck need rope and chains for a tow?	☐	☐
4. Have you seen a fire glow?	☐	☐
5. Can you own the wind that blows?	☐	☐
6. Will a crow grow as big as you?	☐	☐
7. Can I pick up and throw a pine cone?	☐	☐

"X" it:

#			
1.	The breeze blows the sand on the beach.	☐	
	The beast blows smoke at the brave king.	☐	
2.	Spud likes to munch on the low grass.	☐	
	The crow will try to weed the grass.	☐	
3.	Faith pulls a rope on the tow truck.	☐	
	Faith shows her pet the ropes.	☐	
4.	Bing throws a bowl of mush at the beast.	☐	
	Bing likes to bowl with his pals on the beach.	☐	
5.	The gang is slow to pack the boat.	☐	
	The jeep tows the gang stuck in the snow.	☐	
6.	The wind blows the sheets off the line.	☐	
	The teen has a bow on her sleeve.	☐	
7.	The sun shines on the rain and makes the sky glow.	☐	
	When the rain stops, Len will mow the grass.	☐	

Write it, using a word with **ow**:

1. _____

2. _____

3. _____

4. _____

5. _____

6. _____

7. _____

Lesson 14

oa says /ō/ as in g**oa**l and is at the beginning or middle of a word.

 it:

	low loaf load	bowl bow boat
	oak oats toast	crack croak road
	foam from loan	slow seek soak
	row roar road	coat coast coach

roam or road?	stove or soap?
toast or roast?	road or read?
Joan or Jail?	flow or float?
board or beard?	bow or boast?
goat or goal?	coast or coat?

106

Read, write, and "X" it:

1.	foam _____			
2.	road _____			
3.	oats _____			
4.	goal _____			
5.	crow _____			
6.	loan _____			
7.	board _____			

Match and write it:

coat	soak	float	oats	slow
board	foam	croak	toast	load

_____

_____

_____

_____

_____

_____

_____

_____

	Spell:			Write:
1.	p c	oa ow	nt ch	_____
2.	gl cr	ea ow		_____
3.	t fl	ow oa	lt st	_____
4.	g s	oa o	l t	_____
5.	p b	oa ea	ch rd	_____
6.	r n	ow oa	d r	_____
7.	br b	oa ow	k t	_____

Yes or No?

	Yes	No
1. Will you grow if you eat soap for lunch?	☐	☐
2. Can a frog teach me to croak?	☐	☐
3. Can he make a shack with boards and nails?	☐	☐
4. Is there a road near your home?	☐	☐
5. Will the coach be mad if you make a goal?	☐	☐
6. Does a mule get cheese and toast for lunch?	☐	☐
7. Can soap make foam in a pond?	☐	☐

"X" it:

1.	A snow pile is fun to coast on. ☐ The snow pile is slow to melt. ☐	
2.	Joan loads the tube with soap and foam. ☐ Joan loads the tub with meat and cheese. ☐	
3.	The pet eats oats to help him grow. ☐ Oats make a grand treat with nuts and sweets. ☐	
4.	The toad croaks when he sees the goat. ☐ The goat puts on a coat when it snows. ☐	
5.	He rows the boat and wins a prize. ☐ The coach roars at the team as they score. ☐	
6.	A deer shows Ray the best road home. ☐ The toad shows Jay the best way to jump rope. ☐	
7.	Fran loans Will her sail boat. ☐ Will Fran get a loan at the bank? ☐	

Write it, using a word with **oa** in the middle:

1.		_____
2.		_____
3.		_____
4.		_____
5.		_____
6.		_____
7.		_____

Lesson 15 Review Lesson

○ it: stair / slay / stay	green / grease / reach
oak / oats / oars	snatch / snack / such
chase / chose / shows	waist / weep / wait
leash / reach / teach	bunch / blush / blank
spray / sneak / slide	cheap / cheer / cheek

○ it:

low or tow?	stay or stain?
leak or leash?	frame or fame?
sneeze or snore?	chess or cheese?
road or roar?	fair or fail?
beard or bread?	soap or soak?

Read, write, and "X" it:

1.	frame _____			
2.	chain _____			
3.	teach _____			
4.	oars _____			
5.	tow _____			
6.	cheer _____			
7.	loaf _____			

115

Match and write it:

sneeze   snatch   throw   wait   blush
chain   oars   leash   loaf   frame

	_____		_____
	_____		_____
	_____		_____
	_____		_____
	_____		_____
	_____		_____
	_____		_____
	_____		_____

	Spell:				Write:
1.	st sl	ea i	sh de	_____
2.	br l	ai ea	th sh	_____
3.	r n	a oa	r nt	_____
4.	ch th	ea ai	n th	_____
5.	sh ch	ai ee	lt r	_____
6.	f t	ay ai	r n	_____
7.	b t	ou ea	rd b	_____

Yes or No?

	Yes No
1. Will a goat brush its beard?	☐ ☐
2. Does a tame cat need a chain as a leash?	☐ ☐
3. Can you teach a toad to roar?	☐ ☐
4. Can the team win with lots of goals?	☐ ☐
5. Will a whale need an oar to float?	☐ ☐
6. Will she sneeze when she smells the cheese?	☐ ☐
7. Can they load boards on a truck?	☐ ☐

"X" it:

1.	Jean spills grease on the chair. ☐ Jean spills grease on the stairs. ☐	
2.	Beth will snatch the cheese from Brad. ☐ Brad asks Beth to braid his beard. ☐	
3.	The coach lets the team have gum for a treat. ☐ The maid takes the coach home from the ball. ☐	
4.	Lee sleeps and dreams of the fair. ☐ Lee slides on the long stair rail. ☐	
5.	Kay makes a frame for her sketch. ☐ Kay takes the chains from the chest. ☐	
6.	Dale wipes grease stains on his coat. ☐ Ben's oar shines when we rub grease on it. ☐	
7.	Spike roars when he must stay on his leash. ☐ The spike makes a leak in the boat and soaks Jay. ☐	

Write it:

1. _____

2. _____

3. _____

4. _____

5. _____

6. _____

7. _____

120

(Teacher dictated. See Key for Books 1 to 5)

◯ the word you hear.

1.	shame slain shale shave		6.	treat trite trick trike	
2.	chunk crust crush crunch		7.	speck speech sheep sheet	
3.	whoa whale whole while		8.	grate grow gray grape	
4.	bash boast boat baste		9.	bleed bloat bleat blade	
5.	chose cheat choke chuck		10.	three teeth teach teak	

1.

2.

3.

4.

5.

6.

(Teacher dictated. See Key for Books 1 to 5)

122

Read and then spell the word.

1. It is fun to swim and play in the sand at the

   b_____.

2. You must cross the str_____ with care.

3. At times it is a long w_____ for the bus.

4. Pine trees and grass are both gr_____.

5. I like to use my sled in the sn_____.

6. You need s_____ to get your hands clean.

What Am I?

Read and ◯ a word:

1. I am long and thin and shy. I move fast, but I have no legs. At times I scare kids, but I don't mean to scare them. I am a

   > toad.
   > snake.
   > goat.

2. I can be red or green or pink. I am wet and you dip a brush in me. At times I smear, or I am slow to dry. You like to play with me. I am

   > soap.
   > snow.
   > paint.

3. When it is cold you put me on. I keep you dry when it rains or snows. Cats and dogs don't need me, but kids do. Don't throw me in a heap. It is best to hang me up when you take me off. I am a

   > chair.
   > sheep.
   > coat.